The Heirloom

© 2002 by Colleen Reece and Julie Reece-DeMarco

Published by Kregel Publications, a division of Kregel, Inc., P.O. Box 2607, Grand Rapids, MI 49501. Kregel Publications provides trusted, biblical publications for Christian growth and service. For more information about Kregel Publications, visit our Web site: www.kregel.com.

Library of Congress Cataloging-in-Publication Data
Reece, Colleen L.
  The heirloom / by Colleen L. Reece and Julie Reece-DeMarco.
    p. cm.
  ISBN 0-8254-3606-0
    1. Clergy—Fiction. 2. Sacrifice—Christianity—Fiction
  I. Reece-DeMarco, Julie. II. Title.
PS3568.E3646 H46 2002
813' .54—dc21   2002005393

Cover & Interior Design: John M. Lucas

Printed in Hong Kong

1 2 3 4 5 / 06 05 04 03 02

THE HEIR

COLLEEN REECE
JULIE REECE-DEMARCO

Kregel
Publications

To all of those whose sacrifices have touched our lives.

Colleen and Julie

CHAPTER 1

Snow began at daylight. It softened the stark outlines of Spruce Hollow the way flour from Granny Bascomb's sifter covered the scars on her hand-carved breadboard. A few hours later, David Allen stood at the window of the log church he had pastored for more than two decades, his heart heavier than his shabby boots. Troubled blue eyes watched his parishioners shuffle through the snow to attend the annual Thanksgiving Day service.

David sighed, brushing white hair from his brow. The Great Depression of 1929 had closed bank doors and paralyzed the country. Refusing to spare even the most isolated communities, its greedy fingers reached over the mountains and grasped the lives of those who dwelt in David's western North Carolina parish.

For months he had managed to keep up his spirits, and those of the people in his area. Now he found himself bone-weary and hard pressed to be cheerful. How could he ask his congregation to remain thankful when all signs predicted that times would worsen long before they got better? A wistful prayer rose from David's heart up through the rafters. *Father, please help me deliver the message these people need most.* Somewhat comforted, the minister left the window, jammed another log into the glowing wood stove, and prepared to welcome his flock.

Most came on foot. Many who owned vehicles had reverted to walking since the Great Depression began. Even Doc Reynolds often left his Ford V-8 in a shed and rode horseback or used a horse and buggy when making calls.

After greeting the stragglers, David stepped behind the pulpit and picked up his Bible. Touching the lovingly worn cover never failed to remind him of his heritage. Visions of his wild-haired grandfather traveling the circuit preaching, and of his gentle father kneeling with his own parishioners, filled the third-generation preacher each time he held the Book. Just before David's first sermon, his father had taken the Bible from the mantel where it graced its homey, but simple, surroundings. He penned "David Allen, Minister, Spruce Hollow, North Carolina" and the date below his and his father's names before handing the Bible to David. "I hope you will preach from it and cherish it as I have," he said. "It's my most valuable treasure."

"I know." David reverently touched the cover. "It provides guidance and shows the way to eternal life."

"Aye." A bit of Scottish burr crept into the older man's voice. "But it also has worldly value. A line in the concordance was originally printed upside down, and a few copies were run before the error was discovered. Those copies became collectors' items. By happenstance, your grandfather purchased one of them." A reminiscent light came into his eyes. "Father found it amusing. The Bible he had been preaching for years had more spiritual value than anything else he owned, and also turned out to have more earthly value. Remember, if it ever becomes necessary, the Bible can be sold for a goodly sum."

"Sold? Unthinkable!" The younger man set his lips firmly and shook his head. "This Book belongs in our family."

His father smiled. "Your grandfather's dream was for the Bible to be handed down from father to son, as long as there were Allen men. Now it is yours."

A slight cough from the waiting congregation roused David from his reverie. He hastily announced the number of the first hymn, admiring the strength in the faces turned toward him. Faces etched by hardship. Life had battered these mountain folk. Fire, flood, and crop failures had not defeated them, but this Depression . . . could they withstand what lay ahead?

Thinking about the struggles of those he had grown to love, David's throat tightened. To hide his emotion, he opened his Bible. A verse—Psalm 118:24—caught his attention. He silently read, "This is the day which the Lord hath made; we will rejoice and be glad in it." His heart sank. Wasn't this a bit like rubbing salt into an open wound? Could this be the message he was called to deliver? "Hunker down and endure," maybe, but "Rejoice and be glad"? It couldn't be. Yet, he had prayed for wisdom.

David took a deep breath, offered a simple prayer of invocation, and read the verse. A single "amen" came from his congregation. Then, uneasy silence.

The shuffle of feet drew David's attention to the front row. Three clean but poorly clothed Bascomb brothers stared up at him. One gave his pastor a gap-toothed grin and swung his foot. David could see bare toes through the holes in his shoes. A little girl next to the urchin carefully examined the pulpy mass of wet cardboard working its way out of her own shoe sole. David's shabby boots were at least intact.

At a loss for words, he managed to ask, "Would anyone like to share a personal story of God's blessings?" He sent a wordless plea to his faithful wife, Sarah. Unfortunately, her brown head was bent and she missed his look.

What felt like an eternity later, Granny Bascomb, the town matriarch, stood. The wisp of a woman's shoulders were bent from years of hoeing corn when her man was sick and couldn't work. "I do, parson." Her faded gaze swept the congregation. "There's no use bein' mealy-mouthed and denyin' times are bad," she stated flatly. A stir of agreement whispered through the church. It didn't faze Granny. "I say, long as we got our families, church, each other, and food enough in our bellies to keep body and soul together, we need to be thankful."

The indomitable woman's practical philosophy inspired several others to stand and give thanks for the simple blessings in their lives: the completion of a barn before snow came; game animals in the forest; an announcement of a betrothal. David called for songs between the testimonies and ended the service with a fervent prayer for God's blessing. This time the amens were plentiful and heartfelt. Folks clustered around the stove afterward, telling each other it was a "mighty fine service" and prophesying that things were bound to get better soon. If some felt things couldn't get a whole lot worse for them, no one voiced the thought.

After the last person shook David's hand and left, the minister dropped to a seat in the back pew. He felt drained. His parish stretched far beyond Spruce

Hollow, and David conscientiously visited every home for miles around. It didn't matter if the families attended church. They were still his people. He could name each adult, child, dog, or pig that resided in the area. He knew in which fold of the hills every cabin lay, and the easiest way to get there. Sarah often laughed and accused him of loitering. In spring and summer he brought her wildflowers and berries. In autumn, he stuffed his pockets with hickory nuts.

Sarah. The thought of her brought warmth to David's heart, even in his darkest moments. She was undeniably the joy of his life. His lips curved in a smile. God had blessed Sarah with the gift of discernment, especially concerning David Allen. She recognized and respected the times he needed to be alone, such as now.

David bowed his head, seeking the peace that had settled over him in the past, like the warm quilts the women stitched and pieced from leftover fabric. Despite his best efforts, peace eluded him. He finally stood, closed the dampers on the stove, and strode down the street to the building he and Sarah called home. Too humble to be dignified by the name parsonage, it offered welcome to all who entered. The contrast between its warmth and the images in his head of children's bare toes and wet cardboard inserts haunted him.

He hunched his shoulders against the growing cold. Would the snow continue until Christmas or even longer? An icicle formed in the pit of his stomach. It grew with each step between the church and his front porch. David stomped off snow, stepped inside, and placed his Bible on the mantel. He shrugged out of his damp coat and abruptly called through the open arch that separated the kitchen from the living room. "Sarah, what are we going to do about Christmas?" He walked over to warm himself at the open fireplace.

Sarah's busy hands stilled. She left her dinner preparations and came to him. A streak of flour from her biscuit dough dusted one rosy cheek. "I assume we will celebrate Christ's birth as we always do."

Frustration rose in David. "How? In these times, folks can't even afford the necessities, let alone baubles or toys." He sighed deeply. "All four children in the front row and most of the others

"I assume we will celebrate Christ's birth as we always do."

10

will be barefoot this Christmas. Or wrapping their feet with rags." He sank to a chair and buried his face in his hands. "What kind of shepherd am I? A shepherd looks after his flock. It's hard enough to see the adults suffer, but I can't stand seeing the children this way." He raised his head and looked into Sarah's soft brown eyes.

"You are a good pastor, David Allen! Don't let me hear you say otherwise." Sarah planted her hands on her aproned hips and frowned at him. "You've written so many letters to larger churches asking them to help our people that we're almost always out of stamps. It isn't your fault or theirs that they can't contribute more. These are hard times. They're trying to care for their own jobless. At least we can grow crops. Many people in the cities are forced to seek food from garbage cans."

"I know, but there must be some way we can do more." David's shame for complaining gave way to discouragement. "If only we could figure out what it is!" His lips twisted in a wry grin. "We can't cut many more corners or we'll be

the worst paupers in Spruce Hollow. You've put patches on patches to keep from buying new clothing. Young David has picked up yet another job at college so we won't have to send him money. What's the answer, Sarah? What should I do?"

"I don't know." She paused, glanced at the flickering flames in the fireplace, then returned her gaze to him. "I suppose that's something you will have to find out for yourself."

"How?"

The spunk that attracted David to her when he was a young man flashed across Sarah's face. She raised her chin. "How do you usually find out what you need to know?"

"Not by asking you," he retorted. "Even if you knew the answer, you probably wouldn't tell me."

Her trill of laughter brought a reluctant smile to David's heart and lips. Then Sarah sobered. "Even if I knew what God wanted you to do—and I don't—it isn't up to me to tell you. That's His job, not mine." She headed back to the kitchen and her biscuits, leaving David to reflect on what she had said.

He leaned back in his chair and stared into the heart of the fire. How and when would the poverty and suffering end?

CHAPTER 2

David Allen's desire to help his people grew with every hour that rushed the world and Spruce Hollow toward Christmas. He read and reread the words of Jesus found in Matthew 25:34–40.

Then shall the King say unto them on his right hand, Come, ye blessed of my Father, inherit the kingdom prepared for you from the foundation of the world:

For I was an hungred, and ye gave me meat: I was thirsty, and ye gave me drink: I was a stranger, and ye took me in:

Naked, and ye clothed me: I was sick, and ye visited me: I was in prison, and ye came unto me.

Then shall the righteous answer him, saying, Lord, when saw we thee an hungered, and fed thee? or thirsty, and gave thee drink?

When saw we thee a stranger, and took thee in? or naked, and clothed thee? Or when saw we thee sick, or in prison, and came unto thee?

And the King shall answer and say unto them, Verily I say unto you, Inasmuch as ye have done it unto one of the least of these my brethren, ye have done it unto me.

David pondered the passage, especially the part about clothing the naked. He thought of the skinny, poorly dressed children in his congregation. Because he was unable to solve their problems, Sarah's determined cheerfulness annoyed him. Why didn't she understand? He knew he was being unreasonable, of course. Every tender service Sarah performed for her husband showed that she recognized his feelings. And she shared his love for the parishioners. Yet he couldn't help but wish she would offer counsel.

One bleak mid-December day, the troubled minister returned home after visiting an isolated family with sick children. He reached the hogback above town just before dusk, and looked down on the scattered buildings below. Spruce Hollow—such a lovely name for such an unlovely settlement, although the mountains and hills surrounding it were awe-inspiring. As primitive as it was, the Hollow housed people made in God's image. This alone made it beautiful in His sight.

A wintry wind rose, threatening more snow. It chilled his body, but his love for the people, which had intensified since Thanksgiving, made David oblivious to the cold and brought him to his knees. He thought of Jesus weeping over Jerusalem, longing to gather His children as a hen gathers her chicks under her wings to protect them. Was this how the Master had felt?

"God," he cried to the metallic gray sky, "show me the way, if there is one. I'll do anything to help ease the pain and need in my parish."

The wind increased. It furiously tore at his woolen cap and blew through the patches in his coat. It whirled around him like mocking laughter. David fancied he heard "Anything?" echo back at him as a taunt.

He responded to the unspoken challenge. "I will do anything," he vowed. After waiting a time but receiving no further direction, he left the observation point that had witnessed so many of his inner struggles, and started down the twisting road leading to Spruce Hollow.

Supper was over and the kitchen tidied. Sarah removed her apron and settled into the hand-hewn chair beside the fireplace. Flaming logs chased away any chill that dared sneak in from the thickly falling snow. David took the family Bible from the mantel and settled into a matching chair opposite Sarah. Before opening it, he quietly said, "I made a promise today." He shared his experience on the crest of the hill in a few well-chosen words and ended with a rueful laugh.

"I can't imagine what 'anything' will be. We don't have long-lost relatives to leave us riches." He grinned and added, "Any long-lost relatives of ours wouldn't have riches!" He sighed and absently stroked the cover of the Bible. "God knows, this is the only thing we . . ." Invisible claws grabbed at David's heart. It constricted even more when Sarah gasped. Her brown eyes looked enormous, and her soft mouth opened slightly.

David clutched the precious Book in suddenly sweaty hands and leaped to his feet.

"Why are you looking at me like that?" he demanded. "Surely you don't—you can't think . . ." A sick feeling swallowed the rest of the sentence. He fought it back and groaned. "God wouldn't ask such a thing of me!" He waited for her agreement.

Sarah's face paled.

Pacing back and forth, David tried to stem the tide of dismay rising within him. "It's impossible to even consider such a thing," he argued, ignoring the fact Sarah remained silent. "The Bible is our only family heirloom. It can't be worth that much, and it has been promised to young David."

He whirled and stared out the window. Trees twisting in the wind seemed more peaceful than the storm in his stomach. David closed his eyes, hoping to escape his thoughts. Instead, the vision of a kneeling man challenging a skeptical wind danced on the inside of David's eyelids. His promise rang in his ears like a death knell.

"I will do anything."

Suffocated by Sarah's stillness and his own tortured mind, he flung open the door and stormed outside, ignoring her plea for him to put on a coat. "God, You can't want the Bible!" he cried. Only the wind answered. Its cruel gusts pelted David with hard white pellets until he could remain outside no longer.

He dejectedly walked back inside and slumped into his chair beside the fireplace. "Even if I received a fair price for the Bible, it would only be a drop in the bucket. It would never meet the real need here," he told Sarah. She didn't reply, but her eyes brimmed and spilled over. David knew she would not attempt to influence him. It must be his decision.

Long after Sarah retired for the night, David watched the fire dwindle to embers, then ashes. What should he do? Compared with the ever-growing want, sacrificing his Bible seemed quixotic—realistically, what good could come of it? Waking and sleeping, the question perched on his shoulder until a single thought answered it: If Jesus were

A wintry wind rose, threatening more snow.

one of the ill-clad children needing shoes, would you refuse to provide them when you had the means to help?

Two days later, David left for the nearest large city, armed with a stack of old papers bearing crudely drawn outlines of his parish children's feet. He found an antique dealer, and demanded and received a good price for the Bible. Setting his jaw, he went to a dry-goods store and curtly stated what he needed, and how much money he had. The manager selected and wrapped the numerous pairs of shoes. To David's amazement, he threw in a couple of large bags of hard candy.

Happy, tearful faces on Christmas Eve—when shoe box after shoe box was hauled from beneath the popcorn-and-cranberry-strung tree—brought David the peace and joy born of true sacrifice. It carried him through the Allens's traditional reading of the Christmas story in their private home celebration. He only felt a few twinges when he picked up the inexpensive, unfamiliar Bible he now used.

Long months passed, and times grew even harder. Regret came more often. By the following Christmas, the pain and emptiness David felt from the loss of the precious Bible had grown fourfold. "It seems it was all for nothing," he told Sarah a week before Christmas. "The shoes are worn out. People are even worse off than they were before." He sighed. "Let's not put up a tree at home this year. I just can't bring myself to celebrate. We'll have a tree at church, although there won't be much under it. Folks can still come to our home after the Christmas Eve service. We'll pop corn, and Granny's rounding up volunteers to bring cider."

Sarah's level gaze met his. "We will have a tree here as well as at the church." Her expression effectively closed the subject.

Weary and discouraged that he couldn't give more, David dreaded Christmas Eve. He had prayed for guidance on what to say, but no words came. At the Christmas Eve service, he reverted to reading about the birth of Christ from Isaiah, Matthew, and Luke, then called for several hymns. The carols rang hollow in his ears.

Bare toes and cardboard-stuffed shoe soles in the front row increased his sense of failure and reminded him again of the heirloom Bible. Where was it now? Gathering dust on a collector's shelf until some greedy owner could turn a profit? Never had David been at a lower ebb or felt farther away from his Master. "Let us pray," he said. Heads bowed, but all their minister could get out was, "Father, grant that next year may be better than this one. Amen." He paused and dully added for his parishioners, "Don't forget—light refreshments at our home."

David Allen watched his people exchange bewildered glances as they streamed out. Until now, he had at least been able to care for them spiritually. He knew he should be at the party, but he just couldn't go. Right now he would only dampen the joy and merriment Sarah and Granny had planned.

Long after the sound of laughter outside ceased, David slipped into his coat and started home. A dim light in the window beckoned, but he hoped Sarah had gone to bed. He was not going to carry on the family tradition tonight. He knew reading the Christmas story from his present Bible

would not create the warm feelings experienced in bygone years.

He reluctantly opened the door. Sarah sat by the fireplace. A letter lay atop the warm quilt covering her lap.

David's heart lurched with fear. Had something happened to young David?

CHAPTER 3

David Allen stood in the doorway of his modest home, heedless of the freezing Christmas Eve air rushing into the house. "Sarah? Is something wrong?"

Her quiet smile reassured him. "No, David. Close the door, please."

He obeyed, his gaze still riveted on the envelope in Sarah's lap. "Where did you get the letter?" He shrugged out of his heavy coat and hung it, dripping wet, on a hook.

"Granny Bascomb's grandson brought it over. Today's mail came so late, the postmistress evidently sorted it in a hurry and put the letter with the B's instead of the A's." She held it out. "I don't recognize the handwriting."

Neither did David. "I'm surprised you had the willpower not to open it. I know how you love letters."

He grinned at her expression and at her prim retort: "You also know I never open your mail."

David seated himself near the fireplace, tore the end off the envelope, and removed several handwritten pages. After turning up the wick of the kerosene lamp on the small table beside his chair and scanning the first few paragraphs, he stopped and said, "Listen, Sarah. You need to hear this." He went back to the beginning and began reading aloud.

Dear Reverend Allen,
    You don't know me, but I found your name and address in the front of an old Bible. I felt I needed to share something with you and to say "thank you."
    My husband, Lou, God rest his soul, was not an honorable man. Those who knew him best used to joke about him, saying he was the most grandfatherly-looking miser they'd ever seen. His white hair and seemingly innocent expression served him well. He lived his life

by taking advantage of those who stumbled into his path.

Whenever he could get by with it, he paid just pennies for items of value. He connived, cheated, and stole. When he began staying at the shop later and later, I worried he had fallen into more trouble.

I hate to admit it, but I sneaked over to spy on him. I peered through the window and saw him hunched over his desk, examining something by the light of a single candle. Night after night, I attempted to catch a glimpse, through the frosted glass, of what so absorbed Lou. My need to know what he might be up to was greater than my fear of what he might do if he caught me.

About the same time he started staying at the shop late, his treatment of me improved. He was suddenly more like the Lou I fell in love with and married long ago. This only increased my curiosity and dread.

At first I wondered if what he was doing was so bad that he had developed a guilty conscience. I immediately laughed at the thought—conscience and my Lou didn't belong in the same room together.

He continued his considerate ways. At last I couldn't stand it any longer and demanded he tell me what was going on! He stared out the window for a long time. I feared he wouldn't answer me. Then he confided what he had been doing.

Reverend, all during those late-night hours I watched Lou, my husband had been reading the Bible he bought from you.

That is not the end of our story. Because of studying God's Word, Lou attempted to contact everyone he had hurt over the course of his lifetime, and sought their forgiveness. He did all he could to make up for his miserliness, his theft, and for taking advantage of those folks who had no idea of the value of their possessions. He also asked for my forgiveness for a lifetime of unfulfilled promises and pain.

Some weeks ago, Lou fell ill. We both knew death would come soon. Lou had no fear, only peace. He had repented of his sins and knew he had been forgiven. His last words were a plea for me to continue to repay any of his outstanding moral debts.

I was so impressed by the change in Lou, I turned to the Bible for comfort after he died. I also had to know what had brought such a drastic change in his life. The pages fell open to a heavily marked verse, John 3:16: "For God so loved the world, that He gave His only begotten Son, that whosoever believeth in Him should not perish, but have everlasting life."

The word "whosoever" seemed to leap from the page. At last I understood. "Whosoever" means Lou, and me, and anyone else who will dare to believe. I want you to know I made that verse my own, as my husband had made it his. I know I am forgiven and that, one day, Lou and I will be together again.

I intend to continue my husband's work, trying to right both his wrongs and my own. I am in the process of selling the antique shop and its contents, except for the Bible and a few pieces that have sentimental value only.

I will be eternally grateful that you came into my husband's shop. You are one of the few people Lou could not cheat; you knew the value of what you had to offer and bargained well. Yet the full value Lou and I received from your Bible can never be measured. It brought greater joy than I have ever known. Your Bible also gave me back the husband I knew, loved, and respected long before corruption and greed took over his life.

Because of you, I now have many fond memories of Lou reading the Bible. Given the impact the Book has had on our small family, I feel compelled to share it. When I find someone I believe needs the message of salvation and abundant life, as Lou and I did, I will pass your Bible on, with a prayer it may do its work as well with others as it did with us. Thank you again.

—Edith

Never in David's life had he experienced the feelings that flooded through him as he finished reading the outpouring of this stranger's soul. He gently placed the pages of the letter on the table, gazed at his feet planted on the hooked hearth rug, then looked up at the fireplace flames. Words could not describe the mingled awe, reverence, and humility that had come from the unexpected message. Was he supposed to have received the letter earlier? Before he struggled through the Christmas Eve service he considered such a failure? Perhaps. On the other hand, God often waited until His children were at their lowest ebb before sending a blessing.

Sarah wiped a tear away with the corner of her quilt. "What a special Christmas gift! Last year, we witnessed the joy on the children's faces when they opened the shoes and treats. This Christmas, we received more evidence of the joy that has come of your hard decision. God is so good to us."

"Yes." David left his chair and crossed the room to kneel beside her. "This has the makings of a new tradition. Each Christmas Eve, let's take out this letter and thank God for permitting us to learn the wonderful outcome of what I considered an almost unbearable sacrifice."

Sarah took his time-worn hands in her own sturdy ones. "That's a lovely idea." Firelight sparkled in her brown eyes. "I saw your struggle at the service tonight. I know how hard it is for you to read and preach from a different Bible. From now on, every time before you preach, I will put a lighted candle on the altar in front of the pulpit. Its meaning will be our own little secret. I hope that each time you glance down and see the candle you will be reminded of God's mysterious ways—and how He brings good from every sacrifice, even when we cannot understand why we are asked to make it."

David bowed his head and wiped his watery eyes with his sleeve. "Hay fever," he mumbled, then grinned. He turned back to the fire and quoted Matthew 5:16, "Let your light so shine before men, that they may see your good works, and glorify your Father which is

Sarah wiped a tear away with the corner of her quilt.

in heaven." He managed a small laugh. "My light was pretty dim tonight. I had begun to wonder how I ever would be able to rekindle it."

Sarah made no attempt to disagree. She simply raised one hand and stroked his white hair. "I've felt that way, too. It's a good thing the light of truth found in the Scriptures never dims." She stood, stifled a yawn, and started for their bedroom. "Christmas Eve is nearly over. We need to rest our old bones."

David nodded, too filled with emotion to say more. Tomorrow was the Sabbath, as well as Christmas Day. It afforded him a chance to remedy the failings of tonight's service. He would take advantage of the opportunity to minister, in the true spirit of Christmas, to those who desperately needed comfort.

He lingered before the dying fire. A multitude of insights, clear as the icicles that hung outside the window, filled his mind. Thoughts of God's love and blessings came faster than he could snatch up pen and paper to record them. Thanks to God's perfect timing, the Christmas morning service would be far different from the service he had conducted just a few short hours ago.

Notes in hand, David banked the fire, blew out the lamp, and went to join his faithful wife. Of all those gathered for tomorrow's worship, only Sarah would know what had brought about the difference in the Spruce Hollow minister.

He smiled, remembering her promise. A candle lit by her loving hands would sit on the altar, just below the pulpit, casting a secret, reminding glow each time he looked down.

CHAPTER 4

David and Sarah Allen discussed the letter many times during the busy January that followed. February descended on Spruce Hollow with a vengeance, proving the truth of the oft-quoted adage, "When the days begin to lengthen, the cold begins to strengthen."

The snow also descended relentlessly. The twice-daily chore of clearing paths from homes to woodsheds and outhouses kept folks hopping. Icicles large as a strong man's arm glistened from roof edges and grew until they touched the ground.

Early one frigid evening, David hustled back from the wood pile carrying an enormous load of split logs. Fireplaces, wood stoves, and cookstoves gobbled fuel these days. He neatly stacked the wood, then told Sarah, "If I were superstitious like some folks around here, I'd think nature was out to get us. This has to be our worst winter ever."

Sarah finished sweeping up bits of bark he had dropped. She chuckled, a pleasant sound in the cozy room. "Not according to Granny Bascomb."

He joined in her mirth. He and Sarah hadn't been sure if any of Granny's kinfolk were staying with her, so earlier that afternoon, they'd taken advantage of a break in the storm to go make sure she was all right. Even crusty old ladies needed checking on when they live alone—especially in winter.

David and Sarah were glad to find smoke curling from the stone chimney and a reassuring light in the window. Granny's lined face lit with pleasure when they entered the snowcapped cabin. "Well, if it ain't the preacher and his wife! Come in and set a spell."

David peered inside. Granny Bascomb's rocker had drawn the Hollow children like bear cubs to wild honey. "Now I see how you keep warm," David teased. "With all these little active bodies, who needs wood?"

He and Sarah walked across the room to the "hive." A collective, disappointed sigh rose from the circle of rags-clad children seated on the worn rugs around Granny's chair. David laughed and raised his eyebrows in mock dismay. "You don't sound very glad to see us."

"'Course we are, preacher," a towhead piped up. "It's just that Granny wasn't done tellin' us stories 'bout the olden days."

"Yeah," one of the older boys put in. "Granny says this here storm's nothin' c'mpared to some she's seen. Wish I coulda been here back then."

"Nothing?" David pulled his coat closer about him and pretended to shiver. "With all due respect, Granny, Spruce Hollow hasn't seen a storm like this as long as my wife and I have lived here." He caught the disillusionment in the children's eyes and quickly added, "Of course, you've been here a lot longer than we have."

"For certain." Her eyes twinkled. "I calkilate the storm is a mite inconvenient. Maybe even purt' near as bad as most I've seen."

A mite inconvenient? Pretty near as bad? David could barely keep a straight face. He didn't dare look at Sarah. One laugh crinkle around her eyes would result in his disgracing himself and hurting Granny's feelings.

The storyteller wasn't finished. She lowered her voice to a mysterious tone. The children scooted closer to her chair. "Unless I disremember, this one don't hold a candle to the storm forty, no, fifty years ago. . . . Why, the snow got so deep, one man said that when he dug his horse out of a snow bank, he found it standin' on another horse's back!"

She cackled at her listeners' oohs and ahs before adding, "Don't you childr'n pay no mind to such a tale. It ain't and never will snow that hard in these parts." She glanced out the window. "Run along now, 'fore it starts gettin' dark."

Her audience reluctantly struggled into outdoor clothes, some threadbare, and most too small. One little girl chirped on behalf of the group, "Thank you, Granny. We're beholden for the stories." They crowded out the door, shouting that they'd be back for more.

Her face shadowed. "If tellin' tales can bring joy to them poor young souls, I reckon that may be why the good Lord keeps this old body goin'."

26

David and Sarah walked home, too touched by Granny's observation to speak.

⟞⟝

A parting ray of sunlight streamed through the spotless window as David finished stacking the wood. Sarah followed its gleam, beckoning David to join her. He laid an arm across her shoulders and observed the vastly changed world. Evergreen branches bent low beneath their frosty ermine coats. The snow-and-ice-covered yard and the street beyond glittered as if dusted with multicolored jewels.

"How beautiful," Sarah whispered.

David drew in a quick breath. "It is," he agreed. Yet even as he spoke, the scene changed. Angry clouds shrouded the sun. The kaleidoscope of colors disappeared, leaving the landscape gray and bleak. Gaze fixed on the rapidly darkening sky, he quoted the last verse of "A Rainy Day" by H. W. Longfellow:

"Be still, sad heart! and cease repining;
Behind the clouds is the sun still shining;
Thy fate is the common fate of all,
Into each life some rain must fall,
Some days must be dark and dreary."

"Change the rain to snow and you've hit the nail on the head," Sarah told him, a mischievous twinkle in her eye. She quickly sobered. "Do we need to

check on anyone else before the next storm comes?"

David shook his head. "Until the snow melts or hardens enough to bear a man's weight, people in the outlying areas will have to fend for themselves. Even Doc Reynolds can't make out-of-town calls. At least no babies are due, and there's not much sickness, except for the usual winter colds." He stared at the gloomy sky and the few white pellets heralding the coming of more snow. "For some strange reason, I've been thinking about my old Bible all day. I wonder where it is?"

He caught her penetrating glance and added, "I'm not regretting its being gone. I'm just curious."

"Curiosity killed the cat," she reminded him.

"Satisfaction brought it back," he quickly responded. "I guess I'll just have to be satisfied with the fact that God knows exactly where the Bible is, and how to best use it."

Her loving smile showed how much she agreed.

⟞⟝

Winter slowly released its grip on Spruce Hollow. Mail service resumed in early March, bringing David a letter postmarked Richmond, Virginia. He called Sarah and began to read aloud.

Dear David Allen,

I never thought I'd write a parson. It feels strange, but not half as strange as what's happened to me. And you need to know: you are responsible for it.

Sarah's eyes widened. "Who is this person? Why would he make such an accusation?"

"I don't know," David said grimly. "I suppose he will tell me." He read on.

You've probably never got so down and out you'd do anything just to survive. Well, I did. I lost my job who knows how long ago. I left New York for Asheville when a friend said he could get me a job. He said he needed money to make the contact. I should have known better, but was so desperate, I gave him almost everything I had.

You guessed it. He turned out to be crookeder than a dog's hind leg. He skipped town, leaving me flat broke. I ate from garbage cans, cleaned spittoons, and did a lot of things I'd rather not mention. Then I found another friend, one that warmed my growling stomach and dulled my senses.

One night I was so drunk and desperate, I broke into an antique shop, looking for something to pawn. Somebody must've got there before I did. The place was empty, except for a big Bible.

I cursed and started to fling it across the room. What use was a Bible? I couldn't even give that away. Whoever hit the place before me had the good sense to leave it gathering dust, I figured. I finally decided to take the Bible to use for a pillow. It would be better than laying my head on bare pavement.

The next day when I awakened, I was ashamed of having sunk so low, yet more refreshed and clear of mind than I'd been in a long time. I wondered why. A ray

of sunlight warmed my face and brought a tiny hope. Perhaps today things would be better.

No miracles came, yet for some reason, I found myself unwilling to part with the Bible. I continued to use it as a pillow. Sometimes I even opened it and read verses here and there, trying to find out why every time I held it, I'd feel kind of warm inside.

One day I stumbled across Proverbs 20:1. It reads, "Wine is a mocker, strong drink is raging: and whosoever is deceived thereby is not wise." Of all the verses in the Bible, what was the chance of me finding that one? I reread the verse. The warm feeling grew stronger. I knew that if I wanted to keep feeling it, and I did, I had to clean myself up—you know, lay off the booze. It wasn't my fault that I'd been tricked by a scoundrel, but I didn't have to be deceived by a bottle.

I've found a job, peace, and a new way of life. You are responsible. I don't know why you parted with the Old Book, but I thank you with all my heart.

"There's no signature," David told Sarah. He stood. "I wish there were! I'd love to find out more about the letter. It's wonderful to hear the Bible has its own ministry." He reverently placed the letter back in the envelope and handed it to her. "Put it away for safekeeping. Now we have not one, but two wonderful witnesses of God's caring to read each Christmas Eve."

⁓

Shortly after David fell asleep that night, a well-bundled figure stole away from the Allen house. A washtub-sized moon beamed down on the gentle woman carrying a second candle to the Spruce Hollow church.

"I'd love to find out more about the letter."

29

CHAPTER 5

Spruce Hollow was exactly what its name implied: a large section of land, hollowed out and nestled between spruce-and-pine-clad hills that rose to the Great Smokies on the west. On clear days, folks could see the distant mountain range from the top of the hogback above town.

Years earlier, David Allen had staked out his own special thinking place on the hogback: a hidden spot close to the bumpy road that led from the "Outside" to the Hollow. His retreat afforded the pungent fragrance of evergreen sentinels, and their timeless sense of peace, blended with the incomparable view. Many a troublesome problem had been solved in his "green cathedral," witnessed only by the multitude of birds and squirrels that accepted him as one of their own.

There had been no birds or squirrels that fateful day when David promised God he would do anything to help his parishioners. Now, on this early May morning, feathered and furry friends abounded. David's ears filled with their songs and scoldings, the only sounds breaking his solitude.

What a far cry from that winter day more than a year earlier! The resurrection of spring added subtle green shadings to the dark, evergreen hues. Dogwood and redbud trees, azaleas and rhododendrons, displayed tightly furled buds. Soon the Hollow would be at its flower-decked best. David's heart swelled. A wordless prayer of appreciation for the beauty ascended to the cloudless sky.

For a time he simply looked and listened. He remained so motionless, a mother squirrel ran across the needle-covered ground a few feet away, followed by a miniature replica of herself.

A pang went through the silent watcher. A tiny girl with the face of an angel had graced the Allen home for a short time when young David was only two. David senior and Sarah treasured that time. They had instilled in their son a love for his little sister, Alice. He had decked her grave with wildflowers from the time his chubby hands could pick them, and often talked about meeting her "someday, when I go see Jesus."

David smiled. No man ever had more right to be proud of his son. How he missed young David's cheerful whistle! He remembered the day he and Sarah knelt by his cradle and dedicated him to God. Both hoped he would follow the family tradition of becoming a minister, but left him free to choose.

He had. David would never forget the day his stripling son came home from a long tramp in the mountains and announced his intention to enter the ministry. The exalted expression on the fine young face stilled any question as to the validity of the boy's call. It made the good-byes, and his long absence in search of higher learning, bearable.

Young David Allen's two jobs and conscientious application to his studies left little time for letter writing. David and Sarah's constant handling of them wore out his infrequent, hastily scrawled notes. They rejoiced that he continued to stand at the top of his class, as he had done from the time he began first grade in the nearby one-room schoolhouse.

David's thoughts shifted from his son to the anonymous letter. Both he and Sarah had experienced an uneasy feeling in the two-and-a-half months since it came. He restlessly shifted his position. "Father, I feel Sarah and I need to do something, but there is no way to trace the man. We don't even know whether he is young or old, just that he fell prey to drink and it nearly destroyed him."

He hesitated, feeling he was on the brink of a great discovery. His words echoed in his quickening brain. Prey to drink. Nearly destroyed. The man had counterparts right here in Spruce Hollow! Lives controlled by moonshine from stills tucked away in the deepest folds of the mountains. Chief among them was Jedediah Williams, a hermit who had resisted David's attempts at friendship.

The excited minister sprang up like a startled deer. He hurried home, as fast

How he missed young David's cheerful whistle!

32

as his long stride would carry him. Bounding into the house, he caught Sarah's hands in his. "I know what we can do!" he exclaimed.

"Do about what?" Her eyes rounded with amazement at his unusual outburst.

"The second letter." He poured out the plan that had sprung full-blown as he climbed down from the hogback. Sarah's wide grin confirmed the rightness of his idea. In a matter of minutes they had packed a basket with all the food they could spare—including the last jar of David's favorite wild blackberry jam, and a pair of knitted socks Sarah had just finished for him.

A grin of pure mischief crossed her face. She scurried into the bedroom and brought out an almost new Bible. "Do we dare put this in?"

David's hearty laugh filled the room. "Why not? Jedediah can always use it for a pillow!" Filled with elation, he snatched the basket and headed into the hills. It was a "right smart piece" to Jedediah's lair. David returned at dusk, after hiding behind a tree and watching the hermit scratch his head in wonderment at the basket. When David reached home, Sarah waited on the porch, holding another letter.

Dear Mr. Allen,

I was surprised to find your Bible in a vacant room of a second-rate hotel. I'd been hired to clean the room because the usual maid was sick. When I took the Bible to the kindly hotel owner, he said I might keep it. I guess the room had been empty for some time, and he thought that if it was worth anything, it wouldn't have been left behind.

I can't describe the difference that day made for myself and my small daughter, Hope. My husband died a year ago. I didn't have family or friends to help me, so we moved into miserable lodgings. I worked wherever I could. If it hadn't been for Hope, I'd have given up and either starved or thrown myself into the river. Sometimes I considered leaving her on the doorstep of an orphanage, but couldn't bear knowing someday she would wonder why she'd been abandoned.

I hadn't come to the point of taking to the streets, although I considered it for Hope's sake. Each time I was tempted, I couldn't help thinking I wouldn't want my child to know what I had done, or to ever wonder if she'd played a role in such a choice.

I gave my landlord a bit of back rent, and bought what food I could with the day's wage. He told me that if I didn't pay in full within a week, he'd put us out. He sanctimoniously stated he wasn't running a home for widows and orphans. Then he smirked and added, "Of course, if you're willing to be a lot friendlier, I might reconsider."

More determined than ever not to sink that low, I fled to my room and shoved a wooden chair beneath the doorknob. Somehow, I managed to smile and play with Hope until she fell asleep. I sat by her on the narrow cot we shared for a long while that eve. Looking at the protruding bones in her innocent face, and her thin arms, I sorrowed that I couldn't be a better mother. I wished more than anything that I could give her the wonderful life she deserved.

I knelt beside her cot and prayed. "I've reached bottom, God. If You are there, please help me." He didn't answer. I figured He was just too busy for the prayers of a poor working girl. I rose and started to blow out the stub of candle, then I glanced at the Bible. It brought back memories of better times. God hadn't spoken. Would it?

The Book fell open to underlined verses. They were Matthew 6:25-26: "Take no thought for your life, what ye shall eat, or what ye shall drink; nor yet for your body, what ye shall put on. . . . Behold the fowls of the air: for they sow not, neither do they reap, nor gather into barns; yet your heavenly Father feedeth them. Are ye not much better than they?"

It caused me to ask some questions. Does God really consider me better than the birds? Could He love me? If He does, why did He allow my husband to die? What about Hope? How could He let my daughter starve? Jesus is

"It's okay, Mommy; I'm really not that hungry."

supposed to love little children. Does His heart break, as mine does, each time He sees those large eyes in her small face? Each time she says, "It's okay, Mommy; I'm really not that hungry"?

I turned pages, looking for a verse I remembered from childhood—Matthew 19:14—which reads, "But Jesus said, Suffer little children, and forbid them not, to come unto me: for of such is the kingdom of heaven." The candle sputtered and went out, but a tiny flicker of hope kindled in my heart.

"Okay, God," I whispered. "If You really do love all little children, please take care of my Hope."

Every day for the next week, enough work miraculously came to put food in Hope's mouth, but not enough to keep us from being evicted. I didn't care. If God could take care of Hope for a week, He could find steady work for me.

On the seventh day, I packed what few things we owned and marched away from the only home we had. My steps took me to the hotel where I'd worked the day I found your Bible.

Before I could ask the owner if he knew where I might find work, he blurted out, "Hannah? Where have you been? The same day you worked for me, I learned the other girl wouldn't be coming back. I strongly felt I should hold off replacing her until I could offer you the job, but I didn't have your address. I can't pay you much, but I can give you and your child free room and board."

That day I learned God not only loved Hope, He also loved me. Thank you so much for what your Bible did for us.

Sincerely,
Hannah and Hope

P.S. Jerry, the hotel owner, Hope, and I have started praying and reading the Bible together every evening. We are learning wonderful things.

Early the next morning, when David Allen went into his church to thank God for His loving mercy, he discovered that a third candle had been placed on the altar.

CHAPTER 6

David Allen stepped outside his log church. Thoughts fixed far from Spruce Hollow, he scarcely heard the bellow of an impatient cow waiting to be milked, or the music of the morning's first songbirds.

Three candles. Three letters. Lives changed by the message of hope found in his heirloom Bible. William Cowper's timeless words came to mind:

> *God moves in a mysterious way*
> *His wonders to perform;*
> *He plants his footsteps in the sea*
> *And rides upon the storm.*

David shook his head in wonder, closed the door, and started home to Sarah and breakfast. The familiar Hollow smells of wood smoke and oozing pitch increased his sense of well-being. "Although I have to admit I'd enjoy the aroma of sweet rolls even more," he mumbled. His stomach growled hungrily, and he sped up. Whatever Sarah had prepared for breakfast would be good.

David reached home to find the front door shut. Strange. Sarah usually left it open on pleasant mornings. Had she taken ill? He hastily opened the door, walked to the kitchen, and sighed with relief. Sarah stood at the table mixing batter for cornmeal hoe-cakes. Sugar syrup flavored with mapleine from a Watkins bottle simmered on the stove.

David placed his arms around her waist. "Morning, sweetheart."

"Morning." She didn't look at him, but kept on stirring.

Intuition and familiarity born from long years of togetherness alerted him. Something wasn't right. He stepped closer and peered into her downcast face. "You're crying?"

"I can't help it," she choked out. "Every time I think of poor Hannah and Hope, it's more than I can bear! If it hadn't been for your Bible, what would have become of them?" She wiped her eyes on her apron and fought to regain her composure. "I feel so helpless. I want to assist mothers like Hannah, who stay awake nights wondering how they will provide food and shelter for the next day. I can't stand thinking of children like Hope, who struggle to put brave faces on their empty stomachs.

"It was easy to find and help someone like the man who drank, but hillfolk are proud. Many would rather starve than let on how bad things really are."

David looked at his wife with concern. Sarah rarely displayed such raw emotion, even when she was hurting the most deeply. He silently prayed for guidance, then suggested, "Why don't we ask God to help us find someone who isn't too proud to accept our assistance?"

"Do you think He would?" Her voice sounded thin, as if she needed reassurance.

"I do." David paused, surprised at the conviction he felt. He bowed his head. "Heavenly Father," he began, "we ask that if it be Thy will, we may find someone in need of help, someone who will accept what we can give. In Jesus' name, amen."

"Amen." Sarah's face glowed. "Now all we have to do is wait." A tremulous smile curved her lips. "I hope it isn't long!"

"Amen," David echoed, rejoicing at the emerging sparkle in her brown eyes.

Two days later, Doc Reynolds hitched his faithful nag to the Allen's fence and climbed out of his shabby buggy. "Anyone home?" he called.

David appeared in the doorway. "Come in, Doc. Supper's almost ready."

Dr. Reynolds grunted. "Don't mind if I do. It's been a long day." He glanced back at the buggy and lowered his voice. "I need to talk with you and Sarah."

"Come inside and have a seat. I'll call Sarah."

As soon as all three were seated in the living room, Doc asked, "Is young David coming home for the summer?"

"No. He was offered a job that he felt he couldn't turn down."

Doc Reynolds' keen eyes gleamed. "What would you say to letting someone use his room for a few months?"

David's heartbeat increased. Could this be the answer to their prayers?

"I stopped by Sam and Mattie Parker's place today," Doc said. "New family. They live just over the hogback in a mighty poor excuse for a shelter. Came here thinking things would be better. Well, they aren't. Sam's been out of work for months. He's on the hiring list to help build roads for the new Works Progress Administration, but the job won't start 'til September first. They think the younger kids can muddle through, but he and Mattie are worried about five-year-old Laura. There just isn't the amount or the kind of food she needs on the table. She's been delicate since birth. If she doesn't pick up soon, you'll be conducting another funeral."

Sarah's eyes brightened. "When can you fetch her to us?"

Doc looked sheepish. "She's asleep in my buggy. I couldn't leave her there."

Sarah vanished in a whirl of skirts and apron. The patter of her flying feet sounded on the porch and steps, then became nearly silent as she hurried along the path to the road.

David grinned. "I gather you suspected we'd be agreeable."

Doc Reynolds got up from his chair. "I figured that if you couldn't take her, she'd be better off with an old widower like me than starving in the hills. Tom Parker's a strong man, but he cried like a baby when we left."

David's heart was too full for speech. He walked to the door and watched Sarah lead Laura to the house. The child's tattered dress was made from a print flour sack. It hung on her like rags on a scarecrow, but was as clean as hard scrubbing could make it. So was Laura. Smaller than most five-year-olds, her hollow cheeks and sunken eyes made her look much older.

Yet as she and Sarah came closer, David rejoiced to see that poverty had not defeated Laura. A tiny spark glowed in the dark eyes beneath a straight dark bang, reflecting an undying spirit of hope.

"She's asleep in my buggy. I couldn't leave her there."

Laura's arrival was the beginning of a new era for David and Sarah. From the moment she walked into the Allens's home, she belonged. She fell asleep over her supper that first night and slept around the clock. A frightened wail awakened David and Sarah the next morning. They found Laura sitting upright in young David's bed, staring at the unfamiliar room.

"It's all right, child." David swung her to his shoulder. He coaxed a smile from her by promising a visit to a new batch of kittens residing under the porch. Oddly enough, there were no further signs of homesickness after that first morning. Laura contentedly trotted after Sarah, talking up a blue streak. Stories of her brothers and sisters, observations of nature's minutiae, and comments on the world in general, created a steady monologue. Her desire to help was nearly as strong as her conversational prowess. If imitation were the sincerest form of flattery, Sarah couldn't have been more flattered.

Laura copied her every movement. Whether in the garden, the kitchen, or cleaning the home, she jumped in to "help." Sarah didn't mind one bit that her former crisply made beds had a lot less symmetry and a lot more lumps.

"Mister Preacher," as Laura affectionately referred to David, quickly learned to check his once-matched socks before heading out the door. The one time he failed to do so, the front-row parishioners had shared his laughter upon discovering his mismatched socks.

One night, after putting the very-loved little girl to bed, Sarah confided, "I'm not sure I'm going to be able to give her up."

"Think how Mattie and Sam feel," David reminded. "They must miss her terribly. I'm so grateful they were willing to send out a cry for help."

"And that God answered our plea," Sarah whispered. "Isn't it wonderful how He makes all things work together for good?"

⁂

With each passing week, Laura grew stronger. She sat with Sarah at every church service, bright eyes turned toward "Mister Preacher" and the candles on the altar. She'd visit with Granny Bascomb when Sarah went to call. "For once," Sarah told David, "I believe Granny has met her storytelling match!"

If Doc had a visit near Laura's home, she always went with him, but obediently climbed back into the buggy when Mattie said it was time for her to go. "Mother says I'm a brave little soldier," she told David one day. "Do you think I'm brave?"

"Oh, yes. Very brave. Brave and strong and loved."

Summer ended. The Parkers came over the hogback to collect Laura. Tom's new job meant they had to move. "We're beholden to you," Mattie said. Tom wrung David's hand and nodded. Then they were gone, leaving a mountain-sized gap in the Allen household. The quiet walls echoed Laura's absence.

"I wouldn't have believed I could miss her so," Sarah admitted several weeks later. "I just can't get the beds made right, and your socks seem awfully boring lately. I wonder what the Lord has in store for us now?"

David could only shake his head and wonder along with her.

Their answer wasn't long in coming. A politician in Washington, D.C., wrote. He explained that as an idealistic young man, he chose politics, feeling he could use his principles to lead and serve, as others he admired had done. Once in office, the more he attempted to choose right over wrong, the more he displeased those who had elected him.

To satisfy his constituents and assure re-election, he began to move away from what he knew was right.

He struggled day and night. Choices that benefited some, inevitably harmed others. Did slight compromise and bending standards enough justify the possible good he could do by staying in office? Especially when his fiercest opponent was notorious for his lack of scruples? Did the end justify the means?

After a sleepless night, he arrived at his office. A brown-paper package came in the morning mail. No return address. An indecipherable postmark. Who had delivered the Bible? God?

The man sequestered himself and began to read, especially the marked passages. Joshua 24:15 hit home: "And if it seem evil unto you to serve the Lord, choose you this day whom ye will serve . . . but as for me and my house, we will serve the Lord."

David and Sarah sensed the politician's remorse, but rejoiced at his confirmation that the Bible had not come to him by chance. Thanks to the heirloom, he had chosen the high road—and would leave the future in the hands of God.

The following Sunday, David looked down from his pulpit and saw a fourth lighted candle burning steady and clear.

CHAPTER 7

David and Sarah Allen pondered a number of questions in the days that followed, but always came back to two: How had the Bible reached the Washington politician? What caused Hannah to part with it?

"Perhaps she saw the man's name in a newspaper and felt he needed it more than she," David speculated during breakfast one sunny September morning.

"It really doesn't matter how he obtained it, only that he did," Sarah said. A thoughtful expression crossed her face. "Finding counterparts for the others brought us such joy; I'd like to continue the tradition."

David chuckled. "We don't have politicians here, except for the self-proclaimed ones. The old-timers who congregate on the General Store porch hardly qualify."

Sarah's eyes held a contemplative look. "We wouldn't have to choose someone from here. What about writing letters of appreciation—to, say, the county agent or the state representative who tried to get a second road into the Hollow?"

David's imagination caught fire. "I want to write to President Roosevelt." He waited for Sarah's typical gasp and her "You wouldn't!" response to his outlandish suggestions.

Instead she shrugged. "Why not?"

David's mouth fell open when she continued. "He probably won't answer, but he deserves to know people are grateful. He is doing everything he possibly can to help America out of this horrible Depression. It must weigh on him heavily. It's a terrible thing for able-bodied men, like Tom Parker, to be out of work and unable to provide for their families. The president's New Deal sure is helping a lot of needy folks. The WPA has been a real blessing."

"Building roads, bridges, and parks is no picnic," David said. "The President is also restoring faith in the democratic system. Other financially strapped nations are turning to dictators." He picked up his breakfast plate and smiled down at her. "So how's our supply of paper and ink?"

September nights chilled into October. The Hollow blazed red, orange, and gold. David and Sarah wrote and mailed their letters to the county agent, their state representative, and the president. In a short time, warm replies came from the first two, expressing deep appreciation for the simple act of kindness.

The next few weeks subdued the glorious hill-sides to the muted colors of a well-washed quilt. Dogwoods and other deciduous trees shivered in the November winds, their branches stark and naked until snow came to caress them with its soft white blanket.

The four letters on the mantel were well-read. David wondered about his Bible's activities almost as much as his son's, but they received no further reports.

Thanksgiving did come, however. Then Christmas. Conditions in the Hollow were a mite better than they had been in a long time. At the annual Christmas Eve service, David looked into his people's faces. How dear they were to him! Doc Reynolds, a little older and grayer. Granny Bascomb, feisty as ever. And all the others. Yet David's mind ran a double track throughout his Christmas Eve sermon. Memories of last year's starkly different Christmas Eve, and anticipation for the letter-reading tradition adopted that night, filled his thoughts. He felt like a child waiting for a toy.

At last the moment came. David threw another log on the fire. He took the four letters down from the place of honor his Bible once occupied. He and Sarah read each aloud. It almost seemed the letter writers smiled from the shadows of the dimly lit room, and the old Book shed its presence on the tranquil scene.

Hearts filled with gratitude, David and Sarah went to bed. High above the Hollow, the bright stars shone, even as they had on the night of the Savior's birth.

The Hollow blazed red, orange, and gold.

After a milder-than-usual January, February, and March, April brought rain. Buckets and washtubs of rain. Spruce River changed from a friendly stream barely deep enough to swim in during the summer, to a dangerous, devouring monster. Doc Reynolds ordered everyone who got their water from the swollen branch that ran alongside town to boil it. Several mossy headstones in the cemetery behind the church bore mute witness of a typhoid epidemic that had swept through years earlier, after similar flood conditions.

David fretted at his forced inactivity until even patient Sarah could stand it no longer. She ordered him out of the house, rain or no rain.

He meekly donned a slicker and slogged along the muddy street to the General Store. When he stepped onto the worn board porch with its row of upside down rocking chairs, he grinned. It was still too cold for the "porch politicians." A new sign hung on the screen door: "Park your muddy boots here. My old woman's tired of cleaning up what's tracked in." A crude arrow pointed down and to the left, where a pile of muck-covered boots stood.

David chuckled and obediently removed his boots. He stepped inside. Familiar sights and sounds assailed his nostrils. The smell of cheese in a great wheel. Pickles in a barrel. Wet wool steaming from the coats of folks warming themselves at the pot-bellied stove. A rustling sound as the storekeeper wrapped a purchase in brown paper, and tied it with twine.

David returned the storekeeper's "Howdy, preacher" greeting and crossed to the corner bearing an American flag. A plaque designated the scarred counter as the Spruce Hollow Post Office. "Anything for us today, Miss Sally?"

The round-faced postmistress beamed at him over her spectacles. She continued sorting mail into the lettered pigeon-holes built into the back side of the counter. "I do believe I saw something. It'll take a minute to finish sorting. The carrier was late."

"Take your time." David wandered around the room that held everything from peppermint candy and patent medicine to long underwear.

"I knew there was something!" the postmistress triumphantly hollered, waving a letter. "All the way from Boston."

David's fingers itched to snatch it from her, but he refrained. There was no hurrying Miss Sally. She considered it her sacred duty to examine all incoming postmarks. Now her quizzical glance demanded an explanation, but he only smiled and held out his hand. "Thanks, Miss Sally."

She reluctantly parted with the letter, obviously disappointed that David wasn't going to explain this letter any more than he had several others with mystifying postmarks. Heart beating rapidly, David tipped his hat to Miss Sally and padded across the store. In no time he was re-shod and heading home to Sarah.

When he got there, he shucked out of his boots and called, "Another letter, Sarah. From Boston. Come quick! It's taken all my will power to wait this long to open it!"

The first words confirmed it was worth the wait.

April 15

Dear Reverend Allen,

I cannot allow this day to end without writing to thank you. Two weeks ago today, my office nurse handed me your Bible. She had found it on the reception desk. There were no wrappings, only a small slip of paper bearing my name.

A Bible? On April Fool's Day? What kind of joke was this?

I took the Book into my private office and sank to my chair, tormented by visions that had haunted me for weeks.

It should have been a routine appendectomy. It wasn't. The young patient died. I knew it was my fault. Questions plagued me. Had I been careless in examining my patient because of the heavy work schedule I'd been keeping? Was I distracted by the recent loss of my wife? Would my hands have been steadier if I'd boycotted the gathering of fellow physicians that kept me up late the night before the surgery? Had I failed to scrub the necessary length of time and allowed contamination to enter the boy's body?

I vowed never to operate again. I'd come to the office the first day of the month only to turn in my resignation and clear out my personal belongings. I wasn't sure where I would run, but I had to escape.

I touched the Bible's ragged cover and thumbed through the old Book. The gospel of Luke, the Great Physician, drew me. Luke had always intrigued me. A medical man, he unquestioningly accepted the virgin birth. I'd always found it hard to believe. This time, Luke's bold retelling of the birth of Christ shook my faith in everything I had been so sure was outside the realm of possibility.

I took the Bible home. After three days and nights of intense study, I fell to my knees and asked God to forgive me for trusting in myself and my skill, instead of in His Son. A measure of peace came, and with it, the realization that God had truly forgiven me. Yet I still couldn't forgive myself.

I searched the Scriptures, hoping to find a way to put the tragedy behind me and move on. Today I came across Paul's words to the Philippians, chapter 3, verses thirteen and fourteen. They had

been underlined. ". . . This one thing I do, forgetting those things which are behind, and reaching forth unto those things which are before, I press toward the mark for the prize of the high calling of God in Christ Jesus."

The burden of guilt that threatened both my career and my sanity lifted. Paul had brought about the death of many innocent individuals, yet he was able to put it all behind him and follow the calling to serve God. Because of your Bible, I will walk away from my past and dedicate myself to the service of God and others.

Yours,
A grateful Boston M.D.

A few hours later, the rain stopped. David trudged to the church to verify the words of a hymn for his upcoming Sunday sermon. Colors danced across the whitewashed walls. He gazed in awe at the stray sunbeam reflecting light off a rain-touched fifth candle.

CHAPTER 8

Doc Reynolds was the undisputed candidate for David and Sarah's next act of appreciation. The only problem was deciding what to do. "Not a party," Sarah said. "Doc hates 'fuss and folderol,' as he puts it. We'd best just think on it for a while." David agreed.

They didn't have to think long. The next afternoon, Sarah blew into the kitchen like a small tornado. "I've got it!"

"Got what? Maybe I ought to get me some. You're as excited as a hound dog with a treed raccoon."

Sarah looked exasperated. "Just listen for a minute. I found out today what Doc Reynolds wants." She set her sack of groceries on the table. "It's going to take some doing to get it for him. More than writing letters, or delivering a basket, or even taking in a child."

David laid aside the hymnbook he was holding and stared at her pink cheeks and shining eyes. "Some doing to get? What does he want, a wife?"

Sarah gleefully laughed. "If Doc wanted a wife, he'd get his own." She sat down next to him. "I overheard Doc talking when I was at the store."

"Eavesdropping, my dear? Tch, tch," he teased.

She waved it off with a smile. "It isn't exactly eavesdropping when a body is simply looking at yard goods and overhears a conversation in a public place."

David admitted that perhaps it wasn't eavesdropping, then pressed, "So what did you hear?"

"Miss Sally was commiserating with Doc about him being run off his feet tending sick folks this spring. You know she's had her eye on him for years."

David grunted. "Everyone in the Hollow knows—except Doc! It wouldn't matter, anyway. Miss Sally's a fine person, but her twittering is enough to drive the birds from the trees. How did Doc take today's chirpings?"

Sarah sobered. "He just leaned his elbows on her postal counter and said he'd give his eyeteeth to have another doctor around, or even a trained nurse. The work is getting to be too much for him."

David looked at her in disbelief. "He has tried unsuccessfully for ages to find help. You don't think we can provide someone, do you?"

"Not us. The Lord."

"I'm sure Doc has prayed for help for years."

"Yes, but he's just one man. He's never before admitted his need to others. If we add our prayers to his, we'll be tripling the effort. God just has to respond."

She continued. "You're the one always talking about faith moving mountains." She laughed. "If faith can move mountains, it can surely bring someone over the hogback to help Doc."

David looked fondly at Sarah. "When you put it that way, preacher, you don't leave God much choice!" He took her hand and humbly prayed that God would meet Doc's need.

Every morning and evening, David and Sarah sent similar petitions skyward.

A week passed. Two. May transitioned into June. One perfect afternoon, David climbed the hogback and entered his "green cathedral." When he returned, he told Sarah the answer to their prayers was already on its way. She knowingly smiled and nodded.

The next morning, a small, bare-footed Bascomb child pounded on the Allen door shortly after David and Sarah finished breakfast. "Granny'd like it if you'd drop by," he lisped between the gap formed by two missing teeth. "Brother'th gone for Doc Reynolth."

"Oh, dear. Is Granny ill?" Sarah inquired.

"No, Mith Allen. She juth thaid to fetch you-all an' Doc."

Only partially reassured, they hurried to Granny's. They found her sitting in a hand-carved rocker on her cabin porch, enjoying the late spring day. Doc Reynolds occupied a second rocker. A half-dozen children from three to nine years old, all sprigs from the Bascomb family tree, perched on the porch railing.

"Come set," Granny called, indicating two empty chairs. "I got news. Doc,

"I'm sure Doc has prayed for help for years."

"Granny, she is an answer to prayer!"

I hear tell you've been wishin' for help. Well, the good Lord's seen fit to send it."

Doc raised a shaggy eyebrow. "What've you been up to, Granny?"

She waved her letter. "My great-granddaughter Josie just finished nurses' trainin'. She's hankerin' to see what the Hollow's like. Says she'll work for her board and keep here, but I don't need her help." Granny's eyes gleamed. "So if you could use her . . ."

"Use her!" Years seemed to drop from his weary face. "Granny, she is an answer to prayer!"

David's eyes twinkled. "Yes, Doc, she is." He caught Sarah's quick frown, and bit his tongue. The message was clear. The hours of prayer and fasting they had offered as a gift to their faithful doctor friend would remain a secret.

⁓

Another summer passed. Josie Bascomb became an integral part of the community, and an added enticement for the young men to attend church regularly. Fall brought brilliant coloration and the satisfaction of a rich harvest carefully preserved for the winter days ahead.

One evening David cracked and shelled hickory nuts while Sarah mended a worn bedspread. "It's been some time since we had a singing school," he said. "The new schoolteacher approached me and offered to conduct one. I remember leading a certain singing school. Do you?"

"Seems like I do." Mischief filled Sarah's face. "I was a lowly alto. I hit a few wrong notes the first evening. You suggested I stay afterward so you could help me." She gave a mock sigh. "Those blue eyes of yours looked so innocent, I had no idea you had 'designs' on me."

David grinned. "Your father stayed, too, and glowered the whole time we were going over the song. I'm not sure what he'd have done if I'd confessed I fell in love with you during the first stanza of "Just a Little Talk with Jesus"!

He cocked his head. "So when did you first begin to care?"

She chuckled. "Why do you think I hit those wrong notes?"

David roared. "And all these years I thought I was the forward one!"

"I know, dear." Sarah winked at David and resumed her mending.

Singing school came and went. Plans were made to organize an all-day singing convention to be held the next spring. A half-dozen isolated mountain churches were invited to bring their carefully practiced, broken-time gospel songs and food for "dinner on the grounds."

Christmas Eve brought another precious reading of the five letters from the Allen mantel. Five candles continued to burn brightly at each service. Season followed season. Young David excitedly wrote that he had found a wonderful

girl named Elisabeth. They hoped to marry after he finished his studies. David and Sarah studied the gentle face in the picture their son had sent, and thanked God that he had found a good companion.

A year passed, with no more letters about the Bible. The following summer, however, one arrived from Iowa. As usual, it set David and Sarah's hearts pounding.

It was a familiar story: a father who needed his son's help on the family farm. It featured a young man with lofty ambitions to set the literary world on fire—as far from Iowa as possible. A bitter quarrel had ended in separation.

The young man had obtained a poor-paying job writing sensational accounts of crimes for a rag of a newspaper. Then a mysterious package arrived at his stifling, miserable abode in Greenwich Village. Had his father sent the family Bible to show that the door between them remained open?

Touching the worn cover brought overwhelming memories: his father reading from the Good Book at the breakfast table. His mother poring over its pages to find just the right story for the little ones she taught. A sweet young sister scrambling through it early Sunday mornings, trying to find a short verse to memorize for her Sunday school class.

The journalist's heart sank when he reverently opened the Bible and discovered his father hadn't sent it after all. Yet, why should he? It had been the son who had left. He turned to Luke 15:17–18, a favorite childhood story, and read the words aloud:

"And when he came to himself, he said, How many hired servants of my father's have bread enough and to spare, and I perish with hunger! I will arise and go to my father, and will say unto him, Father, I have sinned against heaven, and before thee."

Within a few hours the young man had quit his job, packed what few belongings he owned, and "arose and went to his father." The worn Bible lay in his lap all the way from New York to Iowa.

"There's a postscript," David added after he finished reading the remarkable story. His eyes misted when he read aloud the bold writing that he knew came from the boy's father's earth-stained, toil-worn hand: " 'For this my son . . . was lost, and is found . . .' (Luke 15:24). Thank you."

                —✦—

The following Sunday, David preached on the subject of the lost son. His thankful gaze repeatedly touched on a sixth, brightly burning candle.

CHAPTER 9

The journalist's letter triggered a series of small gifts, which mysteriously arrived on the porch of a local prodigal daughter and her young child. At fifteen, the girl had broken her widowed father's heart by eloping with a ne'er-do-well. A year later, as her father had predicted, the young man deserted his wife and newborn baby. Seeking refuge, the girl and her infant son returned to her father's home.

It took time, but David and Sarah's unwavering support and examples gradually restored both the father's and his daughter's spirits. The Allens delighted in making monthly journeys to the girl's home. David would knock, then hightail it to the bushes where Sarah hid, giggling at the surprise and joy produced by their anonymous gifts.

The Great Depression finally ended. David and Sarah reveled when young David completed his ministerial studies and was called to pastor a small church in Asheville. They beamed the day he and Elisabeth were wed in the little Hollow church.

In spite of the moments of personal joy the Allens felt, there was also darkness and suffering. Many people were still out of work. Europe was aflame—Adolph Hitler's forces rolled through like a juggernaut. Emboldened by a series of swift victories, Germany attempted to bomb Britain into surrender. They failed. Great Britain valiantly fought back, supported by Canada.

President Roosevelt declared the United States to be neutral in the conflict. The majority of U.S. citizens felt their country should stay out of the war, but it hovered over America like a bird of prey.

"We can't be ostriches, burying our heads in the sand and saying 'God's in His heaven, the menace is far away,'" David paraphrased one afternoon, when the radio news declared another

German victory. "If England falls, Hitler will be drunk with power. His desire to rule the world knows no bounds. I fear it's only a matter of time before we are forced into this madness."

David's prediction came true, but it was not Germany that plunged America into World War II. On December 7, 1941, while the Hollow lay white and peaceful beneath a mantle of freshly fallen snow, Japanese fighter pilots attacked the U.S. Pacific Fleet anchored in Pearl Harbor, Hawaii, attempting to cripple it with one massive air strike. Hours later, the United States, Canada, and Great Britain declared war on Japan. Germany and Italy immediately declared war on the United States.

A bleak Christmas passed. How could people celebrate with boys, still in their teens, marching away from the Hollow and into unknown horrors? When World War I veterans—eyes darkened by memories they had long since tried to lay aside—were leaving wives and children, to again answer their country's call?

David watched them go, passionately wishing he were young enough to join them. At least he could help prepare those who were going. He contacted everyone who enlisted. Before they left the Hollow, he visited, offered his support and a basket of Sarah's baked goods, and helped his people set their lives right before God. The servicemen marched away aware of the Allens's love for them, and of God's power and saving grace. David's constant prayer was that the boys would have the strength to endure what lay ahead.

A few weeks later, a message came from young David.

"By the time you receive this letter," David read aloud, "I will be an Army chaplain. The former minister of my church will come out of retirement and step in until I return."

"What about Elisabeth and the child she carries?" Sarah protested.

"I'm sure she'll go home to her folks' place." David cleared his throat and read on.

"Both Elisabeth and I feel I must go. If ever people needed to hear the message of salvation and feel the peace that

"What about Elisabeth and the child she carries?"

comes from knowing Jesus Christ, it is now. As a chaplain, I can help prepare boys to live and to die. I hope I will never have to watch my child go off to war, as you are now doing. Should it happen, I pray there will be a chaplain to offer comfort and guidance. Can I do less?"

Sarah said no more.

Robbed of husbands, sons, and brothers, those remaining in the Hollow were forced to work harder than ever. In a world gone mad, the messages concerning the heirloom Bible stopped coming. The six treasured letters on the mantel grew ragged from many readings.

Tension-filled years passed before World War II ended. Young David returned to his wife, the son he had never seen, and his church. Not all were so fortunate. Most of the mountain boys and men came through the conflict safely, but two new graves were added to the little cemetery behind the church. Dogwoods bloomed in honor of the brave young men who gave their lives to help make the world free. Colored leaves carpeted their resting places in autumn.

Long after David and Sarah had given up hope of hearing anything more about the lost Bible, a seventh letter arrived from Tacoma, Washington—just in time for Christmas.

Shortly after the bombing of Pearl Harbor, the Bible was sent by mail to a young soldier in boot camp at Fort Lewis. He and his wife read it every chance they could. The story had a happy ending. Although the soldier was badly wounded overseas, he came home with only a permanent limp. The letter closed with these words: "Some of the Bible's pages are loose. Others are tattered and stained. We can't help wondering what stories it would tell if it could speak. It certainly spoke to us.

"It sounds like this will be our last letter."

We are grateful to God, and to you." The letter was signed simply, "Meg."

"It sounds like this will be our last letter," Sarah said when David finished reading.

"You're probably right. But it's hard to believe my Bible's work may be complete, even though it is old and ragged." He sighed. "I'm beginning to feel old and ragged too. I wonder. Is any of our work ever complete? Perhaps someday someone will clean an attic, a bookshelf, or an old trunk, and discover the Bible. I doubt if the finder will recognize its worth. It's hard enough for some people to see the worth of any Bible, even one with a new cover. On the other hand, look what God has done with my old Book."

"Yes." Sarah fell silent for a long moment. "You know, this letter makes me want to do more for the families who lost loved ones on the battlefield. Folks in the Hollow are wonderful about helping out after a tragedy, but in time, daily affairs intrude. The flowers and meals and visits stop. Those who mourn are forced to move on, even though they may not be ready. We can make sure the families continue to feel supported."

"I can't think of a more fitting way to follow up on this letter," David told her. "If you'll bake something tomorrow, we'll deliver a couple of baskets and show the families how much we care."

On Christmas Eve, a seventh candle burned on the altar, its flame no brighter than the love in Sarah's eyes.

It was the last Christmas Eve the Allens would read their precious letters together. The following November, Sarah took sick. She passed on a few days later, but her ministry did not die. When Josie Bascomb came to prepare Sarah for burial, she found an envelope addressed to David beneath Sarah's pillow, and gave it to him.

David put the letter in his pocket, and picked up his Bible. Head bowed, shoulders bent, he made his way up the hill to his "green cathedral," brown now except for the evergreen trees. There he opened the letter.

Dear David,

It is nearly time for me to leave you. Before I do, I have a request. Don't let my passing be marked by weeping and mourning. Give me a service of joy. I know it will be hard, but I want to leave the Hollow a legacy of hope.

You and I have been richly blessed. We have learned that the most difficult sacrifices often bring the greatest blessings. Those who attend the service need to hear this message. You know and can share it better than anyone. Make those present realize that weeping endures for a night, but joy comes in the morning.

I will see you in the morning, sweetheart. And remember, I will always be in your heart. One more thing. If I am ever chosen to sing in the heavenly choir, I promise not to deliberately hit wrong notes. I love you ever so much.

Sarah

A laugh mingled with David's tears. How like Sarah to issue a challenge, expect him to comply, and then leave him laughing!

He opened his Bible and paged through. Philippians 4:13 stared up at him: "I can do all things through Christ which strengtheneth me."

David closed the Bible. "Thank You, God." He squared his shoulders, lifted his head, and said, "All right, Sarah girl, Spruce Hollow is in for a big surprise." Then he started down the long road toward home.

CHAPTER 10

No one who attended Sarah Allen's service ever forgot it. The log church was packed with mourners, and a few curious folks who'd "never heard tell of a preacher conductin' his own wife's funeral." The first song set the tone.

Sing the wondrous love of Jesus, Sing His mercy and His grace;
In the mansions bright and blessed, He'll prepare for us a place.
When we all get to heaven, What a day of rejoicing that will be!
When we all see Jesus, We'll sing and shout the victory.

A small Bascomb whispered to his younger sister, "'Tain't like any fun'ral I ever been to. Fun'rals are s'posed to be sad."

She stubbornly set her lips. "I like this fun'ral."

"'Tain't respectful not to look sad at fun'rals," the self-proclaimed sage said.

She pointed. "Preacher don't look sad. He looks 'most like an angel."

Granny's quick glare squelched the conversation, leaving the children—and others—marveling at the peace in their minister's face.

"By now, most of you realize this service won't be following our traditional Hollow funeral," David said when the song ended. "I am honoring Sarah's final wish." He stared at the seven lighted candles, drawing strength from what they represented, then opened his Bible to Psalm 30:5, and read, "Weeping may endure for a night, but joy cometh in the morning." He closed the Bible and leaned forward.

"Sarah's greatest desire was to leave those she loved a legacy of hope. She knew joy would come for her in the morning. She reminded me, and asked me to tell you, that the sacrifices most difficult to make often bring the greatest blessings."

There was much more. No one

present would ever forget the message or the look on their minister's face. He ended by quoting John 16:22: "And ye now therefore have sorrow: but I will see you again, and your heart shall rejoice, and your joy no man taketh from you."

David paused, then said, "We will miss Sarah, but we must remember: The Lord can bring miracles from our sadness. Let's close with one of Sarah's favorite songs." He saw tears glisten when his people began singing the decades-old hymn penned by Horace Spafford, after losing all four daughters at sea.

When peace like a river
attendeth my way,
When sorrows like sea billows
roll,
Whatever my lot, Thou hast taught me
to say,
"It is well, it is well with my soul."

The final words rang. Sorrow would undoubtedly linger in the Hollow, but David's response to Sarah's appeal had lightened the burden.

A few hours later, Young David asked, "Will you come home with us, Dad?"

"No, son. My place is here." Their gazes locked in understanding, then the little family departed, leaving David in the Hollow's gentle hands.

———

Every Sunday, a different family invited David to share dinner with them. First in the Hollow's pecking order, Granny Bascomb snared him for Christmas dinner.

During the Christmas Eve service, David caught himself picturing Sarah's smiling face just beyond the candles he now lighted prior to every service. He marveled that he was looking forward to the late evening ritual, even though he would be reading the precious letters alone.

David considered taking the letters and the seven candles to Sarah's grave, but decided against it. He somehow felt much closer to her when he sat in his usual chair before the fireplace. At times, he felt her presence so strongly, he fancied he heard the click of her knitting needles and smelled her freshly baked bread.

David tossed a log on the slumbering

He saw tears glisten when his people began singing . . .

fire and took down the seven shabby letters. He read them in order. He and Sarah had shared them so often, he could remember where she punctuated the readings with laughter and tears.

He laid the last letter on the table beside his chair, and closed his eyes. "It's too bad young David wasn't still home to share this tradition," he murmured. "Especially since he won't be receiving my Bible. I always expected to leave him the family heirloom. Now that it's gone, he won't have anything."

He looked down at the seven letters. Realization dawned. Young David would have an inheritance, better even than the family Bible. He pitched a log into the fireplace, watched it blaze, then snatched up pen and paper and began to write.

David Allen continued to live and serve his people in the Hollow until he passed on late the following spring. Young David followed the pattern set by his father, and held a service of joy. "How ironic for my first sermon in Spruce Hollow to be at Dad's funeral," he told Elisabeth afterward. "I can't shake the feeling that it won't be the last, though. If God sent me here, could you support me? Electrical power, a paved road, and a small sawmill have made things a little better, but life in the Hollow will never be easy."

She softly replied, "Whither thou goest, I will go."

For a full year the Hollow carried on without a resident minister. Folks wanted young David to fill the vacancy, although, as Doc Reynolds snorted, "How you can call a man with more salt than pepper in his hair young, is beyond me."

Granny Bascomb, edging closer to her hundredth birthday, settled it. "We'll call him Preacher David."

"If he ever gets here," Doc said sourly. "He promised to stay at the Asheville church 'til they got a replacement. They're sure taking their sweet time."

At last, "Preacher David" parked his car beside the road at the top of the hogback, stepped into springtime, and gazed down on his sun-splashed parish. What new challenges would he and his family face? The opportunity to serve those he had known since his youth brought a glow of satisfaction. And yet . . .

David dropped to his knees and bowed his head. "With all this, why do I feel an indescribable sense of loss? I know You want us here to spread Your Word." His last words echoed in the stillness. Your Word.

Understanding came, sharp as the thrust of a spear. From the moment he felt God calling him into the ministry, he had pictured himself preaching in Spruce Hollow. In his dreams he had entered the old log church, stepped behind the pulpit, and opened the heirloom Bible. Now the image was incomplete. Tomorrow he would step behind the pulpit with high hopes, but without his inheritance.

David's eyes stung. Before he could be wholly committed to what lay ahead, he must vanquish lingering regrets. He looked up at the sky and talked to God, friend to friend. "You know how much I always looked forward to owning the heirloom Bible and handing it down to future generations. You also know I rejoiced when Dad sold it to buy shoes for the children, and when he heard from people who wrote about how the Bible changed their lives."

He closed his eyes and allowed the late afternoon sun to warm his upturned face. "I can't believe this is still hanging over me! It's probably because Dad and Mom are gone, and Elisabeth and little Josh are staying with her folks for a week. I feel like I'm trying to return home, when I know it will never be the same."

Heightened awareness of his surroundings penetrated the cloak of peace that gradually enveloped David. A slight wind shook the evergreen branches, filling the air with their pungent fragrance.

"To my son, welcome home."

David had never felt so in tune with God and His creation. He reluctantly left the sacred spot, knowing he would come back many times.

David drove down the steep, winding road. He stopped at the church, putting off the moment he would enter his childhood home. The church door stood open, permitting the acrid smells of cleaning fluids and fresh whitewash to escape. The familiar scene brought back memories: of him sitting in the front pew as a child; of his singing at the top of his lungs; of the times he would nearly burst with pride when his father smiled down at him from the pulpit.

Now he would look down at his son. Could he ever make Josh half as proud?

An attack of doubt suddenly assailed him. Would he ever be able to adequately fill his dad's shoes?

Seven candles sat on the altar. Had someone seen him coming and lit them? They certainly added brightness to the otherwise plain room.

A few minutes later, David reached the Allen home. The front door stood hospitably open behind the closed screen door. David stepped inside. A quick glance showed that loving hands had dusted the comfortable furniture. The shining floor and sparkling windows bore witness of his people's caring. A vase filled with wildflowers welcomed him.

He turned toward the fireplace, remembering its many cheery fires. Well-laid kindling awaited the touch of a match. A basket of newly split logs promised warmth and comfort.

David lifted his gaze higher. It stopped at the mantel, once the abiding place of the family Bible. Strange. The mantel was not empty and bare, as he'd expected. A large envelope sat in the middle. It bore his father's familiar scrawl. "Please put this on the mantel the day young David comes home," he read.

So Dad had been that sure of his coming! David smiled and slit the fat envelope. A packet of letters poured out. The top one bore the inscription, "To my son. Welcome home."

David's vision blurred. He blinked, sat down in his father's chair, and opened the letter.

Young David,

It is Christmas Eve. Tonight, I sat in my chair missing your mother and my old Bible. I always intended the heirloom would be handed down to you. God had other plans.

It has taken me all these years to realize that, while I can't give you the Bible, I do have a legacy for you—one more valuable than our family Book. These seven letters are part of it. They represent a great truth. Our real heritage lies in the choices we make and the lives we touch.

I see you someday preaching from my pulpit, and looking down at seven lighted candles. No one else knows their significance. Your mother placed a candle on the altar each time we learned God had used my Bible to change lives. She said that when I looked down on them, I would remember my lost Bible's good work and be comforted. I pray you will also look down on them, and remember this lesson and our love for you.

I leave you my blessing. Carry on the work of the Master, and never forget: The light you bring is not yours, but God's. I love you and will see you in the morning.

Dad

The new Spruce Hollow minister slowly folded the pages. Before he read the seven worn letters, he had something to do. He rummaged in the kitchen cupboard until he found what he wanted, then returned to the church.

Once inside, he walked up the center aisle, smiled, and placed a shining new candle on the altar.